D0285594

Overcoming Racism

by Rick Joyner

MorningStar Publications

Division of MorningStar Fellowship Church

P.O. Box 440, Wilkesboro, NC 28697

Overcoming Racism

Part I
Racism and the Spirit of Death. 5

Part II
The Power for Healing. 17

Part III
The Two Ministries. 37

Part IV
The Foundation of True Ministry. . . . 57

Part I

Racism and the Spirit of Death

For nation will rise against nation, and kingdom against kingdom, and in various places there will be famines and earthquakes.

But all these things are merely the beginning of birth pangs (Matthew 24:7-8).

The word translated "nation" in this text is the Greek word *ethnos*, from which we derive our English word "ethnic." This discourse was given by the Lord in response to a question about the signs of the end of the age. He declared that a prominent sign at the end of this age and His return would be ethnic conflict. In fulfillment of this, one of the greatest issues now facing the world and the church is ethnic conflict.

The world is losing control of its racial problems. The cause is a spiritual power that no legislation or human agency can stop. Only that which is bound in heaven can be bound upon the earth. If the church does not face this problem of overcoming racism within our own ranks, and taking spiritual authority over it, the world will soon fall into an abyss of chaos, destruction, and suffering of unprecedented proportions—all from racial conflict. As the Lord stated in Luke:

And there will be signs in sun and moon and stars, and upon the earth dismay among nations [*ethnos*], in perplexity at the roaring of the sea and the waves,

men fainting from fear and the expectation of the things which are coming upon the world; for the powers of the heavens will be shaken (Luke 21:25-26).

We see in Revelation 17:15, **"The waters which you saw...are peoples and multitudes and nations and tongues."** In the text from Luke, we see that the **"roaring of the sea and the waves"** is because of turmoil among the *ethnos*, or ethnic conflicts. This will become so great that men will faint from the fear of it. This problem will not go away with time, but will increase. The longer we wait to confront this stronghold, the more powerful it will be. Pressure is now building in almost every world-class city, but when it erupts, it will not be confined to the cities. Even so, the Lord has demonstrated His power to calm the storm and the sea. King David declared of Him, **"By awesome deeds Thou dost answer us in righteousness, O God of our salvation, Who dost still the roaring of the seas, the roaring of their** waves, and the tumult of the peoples" (Psalm 65:5,7).

The Lord will again stand up and calm the roaring sea with His Word. The Lord came to destroy the works of the devil, and He has sent us with this same purpose. We are not here to stand and watch, but to stand against darkness and to push it back.

Racism is not just a demon, or even a principality—it is a "world ruler." It is one of the most powerful strongholds on the earth, and has sown more death and destruction than any other one. Just consider the racial conflicts that have gone on in the last year! The most deadly wars in history, including World War II, were ignited by racism. This powerful spirit prepares the way for, and empowers the spirit of death. The apostle Paul understood that when the ultimate racial barrier was overcome, the division between Jew and Gentile as they are grafted together in Christ, would mean nothing less than, "life from the dead" (Romans 11:15), or the overcoming of death.

The Roots of Racism

There are two foundations to racism. The first is pride in one of its most base forms—pride in the flesh. It is judging others by the externals, which is the ultimate form of pride. In its basic form, pride is simply the statement that we feel sufficient within ourselves, that we do not really need God, or anyone else. This creates an obvious barrier between ourselves and others.

The second foundation to racism is fear. Insecurity is a result of the fall and the separation between God and man. The insecure are afraid of those who are different and those they cannot control. Racism is a powerful and deeply interwoven combination of both pride and fear. Trust is the bridge that makes relationships possible. You can have love, and even genuine forgiveness, but if you do not have trust, a relationship is impossible. Fear and pride tear down the trust that makes relationships possible, therefore creating division.

The cross of Christ confronts and overcomes both the pride of man and his insecurity. The Holy Spirit was sent to the world to convict the world of sin, because it is the revelation of our sin that drives us to the cross to find grace and forgiveness. This destroys our pride by establishing our dependency on the Savior, which also restores our trust in Him. The deeper the cross works in us, the more humble we will become, and the more secure in His love. When we, who are so foreign to God's nature, are accepted back into Him by His grace, it works tolerance in us for those who are different from our nature. Also, those who are becoming spiritual begin to judge from a spiritual perspective, not after the flesh.

> **Therefore from now on we recognize no man according to the flesh; even though we have known Christ according to the flesh, yet now we know Him thus no longer.**
>
> **Therefore if any man is in Christ, he is a new creature; the old things passed away; behold, new things have come (II Corinthians 5:16-17).**

The church, above all others, should not judge others according to the color of their skin, or their cultural background. We must learn to see by the Spirit and judge only by the Spirit, just as it was said of Jesus:

> **And the Spirit of the LORD will rest on Him, the spirit of wisdom and understanding, the spirit of counsel and strength, the spirit of knowledge and the fear of the LORD.**
>
> **And He will delight in the fear of the LORD, *and He will not judge by what His eyes see, nor make a decision by what His ears hear* (Isaiah 11:2-3).**

If we are going to walk as He walked, we, too, must learn to do the same. This is the great lesson of the two men on the road to Emmaus. The resurrected Christ appeared to these disciples and preached to them about Himself for quite awhile. This was Christ preaching Christ—it will never be more anointed than that! Yet they still could not recognize Him. The reason for this was, **"He appeared in a different form..." (Mark 16:12).**

One of the primary reasons we miss the Lord when He tries to draw near to us is because we tend to know even the Lord after a form rather than by the Spirit. If we are Charismatics we tend to only recognize Him when He comes to us through a Charismatic. Or if we are a Baptist, we will tend to only know Him when He comes to us through a Baptist. However, He will usually approach us in a form that is different than we are used to, which He did even with His own disciples after His resurrection. This is because He is always seeking to have us to know Him after the Spirit, not externals.

As the Lord declared: **"For I say to you, from now on you shall not see Me until you say, 'Blessed is He who comes in the name of the LORD'"** (Matthew 23:39). We will not see Him until we learn to bless those that He sends to us, regardless of the form in which they come. Even Israel did not recognize the Lord when He came to them in a form that they were not expecting. This is not a new problem with God's people, but it is a serious one.

The Glory of Diversity

The church is called to have and to be a reflection of the answers to the most fundamental human problems. Racism is one of the most basic and deadly problems in history, and it is increasing greatly in power at this time. However, the church will be different. That is why the Lord declared: **"...My house shall be called a house of prayer for all the nations [*ethnos*]" (Mark 11:17)**. The church has not fulfilled her destiny until she truly becomes a house of prayer for all ethnic peoples.

Paul said that **"...tongues are for a sign..." (I Corinthians 14:22)**. What sign? The sign that the church is to be the anti-thesis to the tower of Babel, where men's languages were scattered, and men were separated into different races and cultures. We see the first great demonstration of this on the Day of Pentecost, at the very birth of the church.

> **Now there were Jews living in Jerusalem, devout men, from every nation [*ethnos*] under heaven.**
>
> **And when this sound occurred, the multitude came together, and were bewildered, because they were each one hearing them speak in his own language (Acts 2:5-6).**

The church is the place where men will be unified again, regardless of race, culture, language, etc. It is interesting that there were "Jews from every *ethnos*" that heard and understood in one language. Jesus is the "Word of God," or God's communication to us. When men see His glory, when He is lifted up, all men will be drawn to Him and will understand with one heart again. The church that truly worships Him will be a demonstration of that. As Paul told the Galatians, in the church every convert, from any cultural background or sex, has an equal standing before God.

> **For all of you who were baptized into Christ have clothed yourselves with Christ.**
>
> **There is neither Jew nor Greek, there is neither slave nor free man, there is neither male nor female; for you are all one in Christ Jesus (Galatians 3:27-28).**

There may be differences in our standing before God in such things as governmental authority, or within a specific ministry, but that has nothing to do with race, sex or cultural background. Even the newest born again Christian can go as boldly before the throne of God as the greatest preacher in the world. God does not show partiality. If we are walking by His Spirit, neither will we.

The Tyranny of the Familiar

The problem called "the tyranny of the familiar" is one of the strongest spiritual yokes that binds fallen human beings, and it continues to hinder the church. This yoke has baffled psychologists, who cannot understand why a high percentage of girls who grow up in the home of an alcoholic father, regardless of the pain and torment that this causes, will almost invariably marry a heavy drinker. The familiar, that is so painful and dangerous, is still more desirable to them than the unpredictability of the unfamiliar that offers far more hope.

It is this same yoke that keeps many ethnic groups from breaking out of their sociological and economic barriers. In spite of all of the talk and the genuine frustrations, most are afraid of change. Why is it we so easily come into bondage to the familiar? *Because we tend to put our security in our environment instead of in the Lord*. To institute true change, a strong trust must be built as a bridge out of our situation. This usually takes more time and effort than most people are willing to give. This is not a new problem. We even see this bondage in the children of Israel when they started desiring the flesh pots of Egypt over the supernatural provision of God. Jeremiah 48:11-12 addresses this issue in relation to the nation of Moab.

Moab has been at ease since his youth; he has also been undisturbed on his lees, neither has he been emptied from vessel to vessel, nor has he gone into exile. Therefore he retains his flavor, and his aroma has not changed.

"Therefore behold, the days are coming," declares the LORD, "when I shall send to him those who tip vessels, and they will tip him over, and they will empty his vessels and shatter his jars."

When the Lord talked about being emptied from vessel to vessel, He was talking about change. This was how wine was purified in those times. It was poured into a vessel and allowed to sit for a time. As it sat the impurities would settle to the bottom. Then it was poured into another vessel and was allowed to sit so the remaining impurities could settle. Therefore, the more the wine had been emptied from vessel to vessel, the more pure it would become. Because Moab had not been subjected to the purifying changes, the "wine" of that nation was impure; therefore the Lord vowed to pour it out.

This is a reason why the Lord often allows radical changes to impact our lives. They are almost always disconcerting. Every time the wine was poured into a new vessel it was unsettled—there was commotion and stirring which would bring out the impurities that were left. Whenever we are thrust into change, many things will begin to surface in our lives. Usually we will see very quickly just how much we have put our trust in the "vessel" that we're in, instead of the Lord. But we will settle down again, and we will be more pure. Change is cleansing. That is one reason why the Lord kept Israel moving most of the time in the wilderness.

The Wine of America

Now let us look at how this applies in a national situation. A good example is found as we look at the problems with the black race in America. Most of the problems of crime and violence in the inner cities can be traced to family problems. A low percentage of black families have a father at home. Many of those who are at home are poor role models. What is the root of this problem? One word—slavery.

It is difficult to comprehend what it was like for a father to go to sleep each night knowing that he could be sold the next day and may never see his family again. His wife, children, or both, could be sold and he would never even know where they went. What would that do to the family? Both the fathers, mothers, and children, could not really give their hearts to each other because of the terrible pain that they would inevitably suffer.

In 1712 a slave owner in the West Indies named Wilson Lynch wrote a letter to the British colonies in Virginia devising a strategy for breaking up slave families and loyalties to keep them from rising in rebellion. He projected that when the black family loyalties were destroyed that the only loyalty the slaves would have would be to their owner.

Lynch declared that when this strategy was implemented it would destroy the fabric of black families for several hundred years. His diabolical prophecy came true. Black women have had to be both father and mother to their families for centuries and they are having a difficult time accepting fathers in their rightful place. Fathers are having just as hard a time taking their place.

If the white race, or any other people, had suffered the same historic problems as the black race, we would be having the same problems they are having now. I have heard many white leaders actually say that we would have no inner city problems if blacks just had some ambition. What do you think slavery did to the work ethic? Such deep cultural wounds cannot be healed without the intervention of the cross.

The black race in America was allowed to be subject to slavery for the same reason the Lord allowed Israel to become slaves in Egypt—they have a destiny with God. When they come into this destiny, the rest of America is going to be very thankful for this great and noble people in our midst. It is the destiny of the black race to carry freedom to a new level. This will be true freedom, with the dignity and honor that God created men to have.

Part II

The Power for Healing

It was by the Lord's stripes that we were healed. In a sense, we, too, receive the authority for healing in the very place where we are wounded, once the wounds have been healed. Even when wounds have been healed, there is a sensitivity in that area that remains. Someone who has been subjected to abuse will be sensitive to others who have been abused. When someone who is subjected to abuse is truly healed, they will not only be truly free, but they will have the authority to carry healing to others with those same wounds.

The black race is going to embrace the cross, receive healing for their own wounds, and start loving white Americans with such a power that we will all be set free by that love. The Uncle Tom of *Uncle Tom's Cabin* truly was a prophetic figure. In spite of all of the abuse he suffered at the hands of his "owners," he was more free than they were, and he was willing to use his great freedom to lay down his own life if it would result in his owner's salvation. The black believers in America, when they have been fully healed, will bring revival and true spiritual liberty to the whole nation.

The inner cities of America will ultimately become the inner sanctuary of God's tabernacle—the place where His glory and presence dwells. The greatest move of God that America has ever experienced will come out of the inner cities. The suburban church may have the gold, but the inner city church will make them jealous with the glory. Those who are wise will take the gold that they have and use it to build a tabernacle for the Lord that is not made with hands, but with people.

America is a nation that is made up of almost every other nation. This is the foundation of the greatness that has been obtained, but it is also the foundation of our greatest problems. Even so, we have the potential to touch something of the glory of God that few other nations have. We have in our nation the setting of another great Pentecost, which required a place where men had come to dwell "**...from every nation under heaven**" **(Acts 2:5)**. We actually have the greatest opportunity to demonstrate the solution to one of the world's most deadly problems. But when our great day comes, we also must be as those of the first Pentecost, in which the church was "**...all with one accord...**" **(Acts 2:1 KJV)**, or in unity. America has come to a time and situation where we will either have the greatest victory or the greatest failure. This powerful last day stronghold will either be defeated on our shores, or it will defeat us. America will either rise to even greater heights as a nation and world leader, or it will fall like every previous great world power. If we do not embrace this glorious potential, we will be destroyed by the problems.

When the Lord described the judgment, He said that He was going to separate the nations into "sheep" and "goats" (see Matthew 25:31-46). The sheep would go into His kingdom, and the goats into eternal punishment. The distinguishing characteristics between them were the sheep were those who, when He was thirsty gave Him water, when He was hungry gave Him food, and when He was *a foreigner"* took Him in (see Matthew 25:35). When the sheep inquired concerning when they had done this, He answered: **"Truly I say to you, to the extent that you did it to one of these brothers of Mine, even the least of them, you did it to Me" (Matthew 25:40).**

One of the primary issues on which we will be judged will be our oneness with those who are different from us. Even the nations will be separated in this way. We know at the end many nations will have gone to a terrible destruction, but we also know that some of the kingdoms of this world will have become the kingdoms of our Lord (see Revelation 11:15). The nations that will be judged to be "sheep," so as to enter His kingdom, will be those who are open to the foreigners.

This is a fundamental issue on which we will all be judged, and it is a reason why the

Lord has bestowed His blessings upon America, and a number of other nations, to the degree that He has. Because racism deals with two of the most basic issues of the human heart, fear and pride, confronting this issue is one of the great opportunities that we have for entering His kingdom. Humility is a basic characteristic that enables us to be open to those who are different from us. It also helps others to lower their defenses against us. Because God **"...gives grace to the humble" (James 4:6)**, overcoming this problem opens us up like nothing else to the grace of God. When we add to this Christian love, being devoted to building up one another rather than tearing each other down, we are building upon the foundation of the kingdom.

Healing Cultural Wounds

Cultural sins are passed down from generation to generation until men arise to humble themselves and repent for the sins of their fathers. That is why we see this prayer so often in the Old Testament, and it is usually made by the most righteous men like Daniel who had nothing to do with the sin. They simply understood this principle and were willing to stand in the gap for their people. This was the foundation of the cross and is the true nature of Christ, and those who would be Christlike.

Biblical repentance is more than just saying we're sorry, or even feeling sorry—it is turning from our evil ways. The white church in the South was one of the bastions that gave birth to demented theologies and philosophies that justified and perpetuated slavery. The Southern Baptist Convention was actually born in an attempt to justify and perpetuate the institution of slavery. Even though the Southern Baptist Convention of today is quite different from the original convention, and there have been many Southern Baptists on the very forefront of the war against racism, there is a reason why eleven o'clock on Sunday morning is still the most segregated hour of the week. There are still bastions of racism in the Southern Baptist Convention, and most other denominations and movements within the church.

This is not meant to point the finger at any single group. The whole church is one of the bastions of this most powerful stronghold of the enemy—racism. That is one main reason why we have so many denominations. However, the church will be free, and Southern Baptists will help to lead us out of this terrible darkness that is now sweeping the earth. The Southern Baptists are on the verge of a great revival, and it will be ignited by their unyielding assault on this terrible evil power of racism.

The white Southern Baptist church should have had the honor of doing what Martin Luther King, Jr. did—taking the leadership in this great battle against the world ruler of racism. Even so, the Southern Baptist church will take up the fight, and will ultimately lead it. The Lord delights in redemption—it is His primary business. He is going to delight in taking what was meant for evil in the Southern Baptist Convention and use it for good, destroying the very evil that tried to use the church in this way.

The Light of the Church

Racism is one of the world's most serious problems, and we must show the world the answer to this problem. However, we will not have spiritual authority over the world's problems if we have the same strongholds in ourselves. We must recognize that the church today is still one of the most powerful bastions of racism. It is one of the most segregated institutions in the world. There are some notable exceptions to this, but generally it is true. Spiritual bigotry is just as prevalent as the natural form. Spiritual racism is at work when we judge other churches, movements or people as inferior, or to be feared, because they are not a part of our group. This spiritual form of racism is a root cause of many of the present divisions and denominations in the body of Christ.

When Paul listed the qualifications for elders in the church, he specified that they had to be "hospitable" (see Titus 1:8). In the original Greek this actually states this as *"one who shows hospitality to aliens or foreigners."*

Basically he was saying that to be a leader of the church a believer had to be open to those who were different. This is fundamental to true spiritual leadership. One who is not open to those who are different is either too proud or too insecure to be in church leadership.

The Nature of Our Unity

While the whole world is degenerating into increasing chaos from its ethnic conflicts, the church is going to become increasingly unified. However, we must understand our unity. This does not mean that we all become the same, or submit to the same organizational structure, just as a husband will never become one with his wife by trying to make her a man! Our unity is based on the recognition, and *appreciation* of our differences.

The whole creation reflects the Lord's love for diversity. He makes every snowflake, tree, and person different. He desires to make every church *different*. However, these differences are not designed to conflict, but to complement one another. It is only because of our continued distance from the Lord, and the resulting continued insecurity, that we view these differences as threats.

This is not to imply that there will be no doctrinal and procedural differences that are in conflict between churches and movements. We must also understand the true unity of the church does not come by compromising our convictions. Even so, most of the differences that have brought conflict and division in the church are not serious enough for us to divide over. In many cases, we are resisting the most those whom we need the most, to give *proper* balance and perspective to our vision of the truth.

In my twenty plus years in the church I have never witnessed a single division that was truly based on a genuine commitment to truth. Men may have used doctrine or procedure as an excuse, but the real reason behind every split that I have witnessed was territorial preservation—a most deadly and selfish evil in the church, and a major foundation of our spiritual racism. Racism empowers the spirit of death, and this spirit has probably killed more churches and movements than any other enemy. Until we are free of this enemy we will not have spiritual authority over it in human affairs. The only answer for us and the world is the cross. At the cross the dividing walls are taken down and we are free to come into a true unity.

One of the most significant racial barriers in the world today is between men and women. A man will never become the true man that he was created to be until he learns to properly relate to women, recognizing and appreciating their differences. Men will not have a true perspective of the world, or anything else, including the Lord, until we are open to the perspective that women have. The same is true for women. Therefore, to walk in truth, we need each other. A woman will never be the lady that she has been created to be without learning to relate to men properly. There are deep wounds remaining on the part of each, but there is healing for all of them at the cross. There is no true healing anywhere else.

No Charismatic, Pentecostal, Baptist, Methodist or any other will fulfill his own destiny without a proper relationship to the rest of the church. Even though the high priest of Israel was from the Tribe of Levi, he carried the stones that represented all of the different tribes on his chest. This was to symbolize that those who would walk in the high calling must carry all of God's people on their hearts.

Only when we have been delivered from our own spiritual ethnic conflicts will we become **"...a house of prayer for all nations."** **(Isaiah 56:7 NKJV)** That is our fundamental calling. The times are about to press us into the desperation that is obviously required for us to do this. Let us not waste a day. Those who do not overcome the world will be overcome by it. When we begin to carry the cross, there is no spirit in this world that will not be subject to us. The cross has overcome the world, and, when we embrace it, we too will overcome the world.

We will never have true unity until we can see each other with the Lord's eyes, hear each other with His ears, and love each other with His heart. Every human problem in the world is impossible for men to overcome until they embrace the cross. But how can we expect men to do this until we, the church, have done it? We can only bear true spiritual fruit to the degree that we are abiding in the Vine. The stronger our union is with Him, the more fruit we will bear.

The Lord Jesus did not judge by what He saw with His natural eyes, or heard with His natural ears. His judgment was determined by what the Father revealed to Him. We cannot expect to walk in truth if we continue to get our discernment from the secular press, the evening news, or even what we see with our own eyes at times. There is always a story behind the story that only God knows, but He will reveal it to us if we turn to Him for our understanding.

Love and Revelation

In Deuteronomy 10:18-19, the Israelites were commanded to love the alien who was in their midst. In chapter 31, verse 12 they were commanded to teach the alien. There is a great revelation in this—*we must love someone before we can teach them*. Again, true spiritual authority is founded upon love.

America is the greatest power on earth. It is also probably the most respected overall, and the most emulated. At the same time, it is also probably the most despised nation on earth. This hatred of America is not just jealousy. There is some basis to this hatred. It may almost entirely be unintentional, but we are continually offending and insulting other cultures. We, who are a nation that has been truly made up of those from every other nation, should be the last one to do this.

At last count almost sixty prime ministers and leaders of other nations have been educated in the United States, yet a high percentage of these were anti-American in their policy. The Japanese military leader who planned the attack on Pearl Harbor, and the admiral who commanded the attack force, were both educated at Harvard University! How could history have been changed if we had treated these men differently?

Between 200,000 and 300,000 foreigners are presently being educated in the United States. They are usually the "cream of the crop" of their nation. Many of them are from nations where it is against the law to preach the gospel. We can reach the world without even leaving home, just by showing hospitality to the foreigners who are presently on our campuses. They are usually isolated and lonely. Many of them have nowhere to go during holidays. Because of this, their time in the United States is a negative experience. Many of them will one day be the leaders of their nations—some even Prime Ministers or Foreign Ministers. If the churches around these campuses would just reach out to these foreigners, the world could be greatly impacted.

The Ultimate Racist Barrier

The ultimate racist barrier, with regard to spiritual power, is the barrier between Jew and Gentile. This is by God's design. The Jew is the natural seed of Abraham, and the church is the spiritual seed. Together they are meant to represent the heavens and the earth, which is why the promise to Abraham was that his seed would be as **"...the stars of the heavens, and as the sand which is on the seashore..." (Genesis 22:17).** When the barrier between Jew and Gentile is overcome, it will signal the overcoming of the gulf between the spiritual and earthly realm, so that God, who is Spirit, may establish His eternal habitation with man.

The Jew is the embodiment of the humanistic spirit. They are a barometer of humanity—embattled within and without. As Paul said, **"From the standpoint of the gospel they are enemies *for your sake..."* (Romans 11:28).** They were hardened, or made hard to reach, *for the sake of the gospel.* That is, the Jew represents the "acid test" of our message. Until we have a gospel that will make the Jew jealous, we do not really have the goods yet. That is why we are exhorted to preach the gospel to the Jew first. When we preach to the Jew we will quickly find out the quality of our message.

The wounds that have been inflicted upon the Jews by the church are some of the most deep and tragic in history. We have made our job much more difficult. It will take an unprecedented humility on the part of the church, which will enable the Lord to extend an unprecedented grace and trust us with an unprecedented anointing, to reach the Jews. That was precisely God's plan. We cannot fulfill our commission as the church without the Jews. They must be grafted back in. But that which requires this unprecedented anointing will have brought the church to a place of such unprecedented humility and grace, that every racist barrier within us will have been overcome. That is why Paul could so confidently affirm that, when this happened, it would release the ultimate grace on mankind: **"For if their rejection be the reconciliation of the world, what will their acceptance be but life from the dead?" (Romans 11:15).** The spirit of death, and the racism that empowers it, will be overcome when the Jew and Gentile have been grafted into the Vine together.

The New Creation

The time period in which the Lord dealt almost exclusively with the Jews was about 2,000 years. The time of the Gentiles has now been about 2,000 years. What we are now coming into is not another time of the Jews, but of the Jew and the Gentile grafted into one new creation through Christ.

True unity is in diversity, not in conformity. Converted Israel will not be like the church. The church is very far from being what God created her to be, and so is Israel. When they are truly joined together, neither will be like they are now. We desperately need what the born-again Jew is going to bring into the church. This does not imply a returning to the Law, but the church has not yet demonstrated on earth what the true new creation is. This union of the natural and spiritual seed of Abraham is required before it can be done. This is the best wine, which the Lord has saved for last.

Many in the church have embraced a "replacement theology," which replaces all of the present purposes of God for Israel with the church. Others have embraced a "replacement, replacement theology" which replaces the church with Israel. Both cloud this ultimate purpose for Israel and the church. In the book of Romans, which is the most explicit book of New Covenant theology in the Scriptures, Paul clearly established God's purpose for each. He also warned against becoming **"...arrogant toward the** [natural] **branches..." (11:18),** adding, **"...Do not be conceited, but fear; for if God did not spare the natural branches, neither will He spare you" (11:20-21).** This is an issue of such importance that it can cut us off from God's purpose.

This does not imply that we must accept everything Israel does. It is also clearly unbiblical that the Jews can be grafted into the purpose of God in any way except through Christ. But speaking of the natural branches, Paul declared: **"I say then, God has not rejected His people, has He? May it never be!..." (Romans 11:1).** For God to reject natural Israel would be to impugn the very integrity of His promises made to Abraham and throughout the entire Old Testament, most of which there is no way to attribute to anyone but the natural Jew. As Paul asserted:

> **Then what advantage has the Jew? Or what is the benefit of circumcision?**
>
> ***Great in every respect.* First of all, that they were entrusted with the oracles of God.**
>
> **What then? If some did not believe, their unbelief will not nullify the faithfulness of God, will it?**
>
> **May it never be! Rather, let God be found true, though every man be found a liar, as it is written (Romans 3:1-4).**
>
> **From the standpoint of God's choice they are beloved for the sake of the fathers;**
>
> **for the gifts and the calling of God are irrevocable.**

For just as you once were disobedient to God, but now have been shown mercy because of their disobedience,

so these also now have been disobedient, in order that because of the mercy shown to you they also may now be shown mercy.

For God has shut up all in disobedience *that He might show mercy to all* (11:28-32).

It will take extraordinary humility for the church to fully see God's purpose in natural Israel, and it will take the same degree of humility for natural Israel to see God's purpose in the church. But it will happen, and when it does it will release an unprecedented measure of God's grace to both.

Many believe that only converted Jews will be able to reach the Jews. This is contrary to His purpose, as well as to the biblical testimony of how God reaches people. It was for this reason that the Lord sent Peter to the Jews and Paul to the Gentiles. According to our modern mentality, the Lord got this wrong. Certainly Paul, the Pharisee of Pharisees, would be better able to relate to the Jews. And Peter, the simple fisherman, would obviously be better able to reach the Gentiles. In the natural this is true, but our gospel is not natural, it is spiritual, and the natural mind still cannot comprehend it.

The Lord sent Paul to the Gentiles *because* he was an offense to them. Therefore, the only way Paul could fulfill his commission was to be utterly dependent on the Holy Spirit—which is the only way the gospel is truly empowered. Likewise, the only way Peter could reach the Jews was to be utterly dependent on the Holy Spirit. This is true of all of us! Natural affinities do not help the gospel; they usually get in the way. **"That which is born of the flesh is flesh, and that which is born of the Spirit is spirit" (John 3:6).**

Just as the Lord humbled the Gentiles by sending them Jews, He is going to humble the Jews by sending them Gentiles. Of course some Jews will have some success in reaching their people, but generally this will not be the way they are reached. It is understandable that the heart of the Jewish convert longs to reach his own people, just as Paul's did to the point where he was even willing to give up his own salvation. Even so, Paul could not reach the Jews because that was not his commission. The Gentile church needs to take up the burden of reaching the Jews, and we desperately need the converted Jews to go to the church.

The Distortion of Reality

The news media is one of the primary tools being used by the enemy to sow deception and division between peoples. Although this may not be their intent, it is the effect. The news itself is a gross distortion of reality. Only the most extreme events make the news, and most of them are acts of violence and destruction. Good news does not sell, but even the good that makes the news is not a true perception of reality. News of domestic violence is never balanced by news of the many happy families. The overwhelming majority of Americans will today do their jobs and go about their business in a normal manner, but none of that, which is "normal" America, will make the evening news. The news itself presents a very distorted caricature of life in America, or anywhere else.

Even the Christian media, trying to do an honest job of reporting interesting events in the church, often creates an unreal perception of Christianity for their own Christian readers. The average church in America is not like the churches that are newsworthy, but the day by day ministries of the average church in their communities are probably doing far more to accomplish a true advance for the gospel. These average churches are also a more accurate reflection of the true state of Christianity today, for good or for bad.

Even when there is no intention to distort, the very nature of the modern media distorts reality. Even family-oriented sitcoms project families where almost every action or statement is either cute, funny, or dramatic. The truly normal family would make a very boring sitcom. When the average family compares their lives to those of the television family they often become disappointed with what they have, and who they are. The overall effect of this is to blur reality and to reduce our perceptions to "sound bites," having been subtly trained only to respond to extremes.

Srongholds are basically lies that people believe. The more people that believe a falsehood, the more powerful that stronghold will be. The enemy is using the media to sow a demented perception of almost everything. The result will be that more and more of the extremes projected by the media will become normal behavior. Only the church, which has been given the Spirit of Truth, has the grace and power required to tear down these strongholds of misconception and false judgments. The divinely powerful weapons that we have been trusted with were given to us for the purpose of tearing down strongholds, and we must use them.

The Deception of Extremes

One of Satan's greatest successes in bringing and maintaining division between people has been to keep us judging other people groups by their most extreme elements. In this way liberals look at conservatives and see the KKK. Conservatives look at liberals and see communists. It is a primary strategy of the enemy to have us perceiving one another through caricatures that the enemy has sown in the minds of the people. This drives us farther apart and decreases the possibility of unity that the enemy fears so much.

Few Christians today are of the nature that was demonstrated by the crusaders, but the world does tend to view us all according to the most extreme elements of the faith. We must also recognize that very few members of other religions, or ethnic groups, are like the most extreme elements which we probably have viewed in the media.

Because the enemy's basic strategy is to sow division and misunderstanding by having us judge each other after projected images and caricatures, we must overcome this by learning to judge other people after the Spirit and not after the flesh. We must not continue to receive our discernment, and in many cases, even our information, from the media, but from the Holy Spirit.

Part III

The Two Ministries

The Scriptures reveal that there are two acts which go on continually before the throne of God—*intercession* and *accusation*. The conflict between these two is a focal point of the battle between the kingdom of God and the kingdom of darkness. Because God has chosen to make the church His dwelling place, and therefore the place of His throne, it is in the heart of the church that this battle now rages.

Jesus "**...always lives to make intercession...**" (**Hebrews 7:25**). It is the fundamental nature of Jesus to be an intercessor, a priest. To the degree that we abide in Him, Jesus will use us to intercede. For this reason, His church is called to be a "**...house of prayer for all the nations...**" (**Mark 11:17**).

Satan is called "**the accuser of our brethren...who accuses them before our God day and night**" (**Revelation 12:10**). To the degree that the enemy has access to our lives he will use us to accuse and criticize the brethren. Like the two trees in the garden, we must all choose which of these we are going to partake.

We may ask how Satan could continue to accuse the saints before God if he has been thrown out of heaven and no longer has access to the throne. The answer is that Satan uses the saints, who do have access to the throne, to do this diabolical work for him.

Satan's Greatest Victory

Satan is called by many titles but certainly his most effective guise has been "the accuser of the brethren." This title was given to him because of his effectiveness in getting brother to turn against brother. From the time he entered the garden to thwart the purpose of man, this has been his specialty. Even when there were just two brothers on earth they could not get along. The presence of Satan will always promote discord and division.

Satan's greatest victory over the church is in turning brethren against each other. *Accusation* has been his most effective and deadly tool in destroying the light, the power, and the witness of the body of Christ. Our ability to accomplish our purpose in this world will be determined by the degree to which we can dispel our deadly enemy and learn to live for one another.

The greatest threat to Satan's domain is the unity of the church. The devil knows very well the awesome authority that Jesus has given to any two that will agree. He knows that with agreement between just two saints the Father will give them what they ask. He understands that one saint can put a thousand to flight but two of them together can put ten thousand to flight. Unity does not just increase our spiritual authority—it exponentially multiplies it. Unfortunately, the enemy has understood all of this much better than the church has.

The access the accuser has to most believers is through their insecurity. This drives them to become territorial or possessive. The insecure are threatened by anything they cannot control. The accuser may use many seemingly noble justifications for his attacks on others, such as to protect the truth or the sheep, but rarely is there a division in the church that was not rooted in territorial or self-preservation. The greater the authority or influence that one has in the church, the bigger the target they make. Satan knows well that if he can sow territorial or self-preservation in the heart of a spiritual leader, the leader will sow it in all of those under him, and the more destructive the division or sectarian spirit will be.

Ironically, the resulting division that is caused by trying to protect our domains is the very thing that cuts us off from true spiritual authority and anointing. This ultimately results in our losing the very thing we are so desperately trying to preserve, which is an incontrovertible law of the spirit: **"For whoever wishes to save his life shall lose it; but whoever loses his life for My**

sake shall find it" (Matthew 16:25). Isaiah addressed this issue in Isaiah 58:8-9:

> **Then your light will break out like the dawn, and your recovery will speedily spring forth; and your righteousness will go before you; the glory of the LORD will be your rear guard.**
>
> **Then you will call, and the LORD will answer; you will cry, and He will say, "Here I am."** *IF* **you remove the yoke from your midst, the pointing of the finger, and speaking wickedness (verses 8-9).**

We are promised that if we remove the yoke of criticism from our midst, which is portrayed as **"the pointing of the finger, and speaking wickedness,"** we are promised that our light will break out, our healing will come speedily, the glory of the Lord will follow us, and He will answer our prayers. There is possibly nothing that can so radically change the church, and the lives of individual believers, than having our criticisms changed into intercession. Likewise, it is probable that the addiction to criticism is the main reason why there is so little light, so little healing, so little of the glory of the Lord, and so little answered prayer in the church today.

Criticism Is Pride

Criticism is one of the ultimate manifestations of pride because, whenever we criticize someone else, we are by that assuming we are superior to them. Pride brings that which any rational human being should fear the most—God's resistance. **"...God resists the proud, but gives grace to the humble" (James 4:6 NKJV).** We would be better off having all of the demons in hell resisting us than God!

Pride caused the first fall and it has been a root in probably every fall from grace since. Peter's betrayal of the Lord is one of the great examples of how pride causes us to fall from grace. On that same night when Peter betrayed the Lord, he had earlier charged a Roman cohort to defend his Lord. Even though this was misguided zeal, it was impressive courage—a Roman cohort was composed of 800 men! However, when the Lord warned Peter of his impending denial of Him, Peter had challenged the Son of God Himself, declaring that "They may all fall away from you but not me." Peter knew that he was a man of courage, and would be willing to die for the Lord, he just did not know where the courage came from. The Lord did not cause Peter to fall that night; He just removed the grace by which he was standing. Then the fearless man who had charged a Roman cohort could not even stand before a servant girl!

None of us can stand at any point except by the grace of God. This is more than a cliché—it is a basic biblical truth. When we condemn others who are having problems because we are not, we are putting ourselves in jeopardy of falling to the same sins. That is why Paul warned us: **"Brethren, even if a man is caught *in any trespass*, you who are spiritual, restore such a one in a spirit of gentleness; each one looking to yourself, *lest you too be tempted*"** (Galatians 6:1).

Who Are We Criticizing?

When we criticize another Christian we are actually saying that God's workmanship does not meet up to our standards, that we could do it better. When we criticize someone else's children, who will take offense? The parents! This is no less true with God. When we judge one of His people we are judging Him. When we judge one of His leaders we are really judging His leadership—by that we are saying He does not know what He is doing with the leadership He is providing.

Such grumbling and complaining is the same problem that kept the first generation of the children of Israel from possessing their promised land. Their grumbling caused them to spend their entire life wandering in dry places, and this is the chief reason why so many Christians do not walk in the promises of God. We have been warned:

> **Do not speak against one another, brethren. He who speaks**

against a brother, or judges his brother, speaks against the law, and judges the law; but if you judge the law, you are not a doer of the law, but a judge of it.

There is only one Lawgiver and Judge, the One who is able to save and to destroy [when we judge the law, we judge the Lawgiver]; but who are you who judge your neighbor? (James 4:11-12).

When we "point the finger" to criticize, we yoke ourselves:

Judge not, that you be not be judged.

For with what judgment you judge, you will be judged; and with the measure you use, it will be measured back to you (Matthew 7:1-2 NKJV).

The Spirit of Poverty

I once visited a state that was under one of the most powerful spirits of poverty that I have witnessed in this country. This was remarkable because it was a state of great beauty and natural resources, and with talented and resourceful people. However, another characteristic of the people there also stood out—they seemed to inevitably scorn and criticize the prosperous or powerful. With every pastor of a small church that I met (and almost all of them in this state were very small), the conversation would inevitably turn to criticizing "mega churches" and "mega ministries," who these people obviously thought were the reason for their own problems. This was even sadder because many of these small church pastors were more anointed and called to walk in more spiritual authority than the leaders of the mega churches, or ministries, that they criticized; but their judgments had restrained the grace of God in their lives.

It is biblically established that we may sometimes be abased and sometimes we need to abound. The apostle Paul even claimed to have gone hungry at times, and he sternly warned us to be content when we just have food and covering (see I Timothy 6:8). However, if I am to be abased, I want to do it in submission to God and to what He is trying to work in my life, not in submission to an evil spirit of poverty. I certainly do not want to be yoked to poverty because of my own evil judgments of others.

Many pastors yoke themselves, and their congregations, to financial poverty by criticizing how other men of God take up offerings. Because of their judgments they cannot even take up a biblical offering without feeling guilty. As the text in Isaiah 58 implies, the primary reason for the darkness, lack of healing, unanswered prayer, and lack of the glory of God, is our own critical spirit. Of the many people I have met with exceptional mantles of spiritual authority, but who were lacking in spiritual fruit, this seemed to always be a prevailing characteristic in their lives. They had judged and criticized the ministries of others who were gaining influence, and had thereby disqualified themselves from the grace of God in that area. Our criticisms will bring us to poverty. **"Death and life are in the power of the tongue, and those who love it will eat its fruit" (Proverbs 18:21).**

As Solomon observed:

But the path of the just is like the shining sun, that shines ever brighter unto the perfect day.

The way of the wicked is like darkness; they do not know what makes them stumble (Proverbs 4:18-19 NKJV).

If we are walking in righteousness we will be walking in increasing light. Those who stumble around in the dark seldom know the reason for that darkness, or they would not be in it. However, the critical person is usually critical of everyone but himself, and therefore he cannot see his own problems. As the Lord stated, he is so busy looking for specks in the eyes of his brothers that he cannot see the big log in his own eye, which is the reason for his blindness.

Stumbling Blocks

The Lord indicated that the very last thing that we should ever want to be is a stumbling block. He said it would be better for us not to have been born than to cause even one of His little ones to stumble. In the same conversation in which He warned us not to become a stumbling block, (see Matthew 18), He gave clear instructions about how we are to deal with a brother or sister who is in sin so that we will not become a stumbling block. First, we must go to the person *in private*. Only after he has rejected our counsel do we go to him with another brother.

Only after he has rejected both should we ever go before the rest of the church with the issue. If we do not follow this pattern we will be in jeopardy of suffering a fate worse than the person who is in sin—becoming a stumbling block (see Matthew 18:15-17).

This tendency toward unrighteous judgment in the church is very possibly why many will come to the Lord on the judgment day, having done many great things in His name, but will still hear those terrible words: **"Depart from Me, you who practice lawlessness" (Matthew 7:23).** By the Lord's own teachings it would be very hard for us to overstate the importance of this terrible sin of unrighteous judgment.

I have heard numerous excuses for not following this pattern for dealing with sin in

Matthew 18, such as: "I knew they would not listen to me," or "If they have a public ministry we have a right to expose them publicly." However, the Lord did not say that we only had to comply with His instructions when we knew people would listen to us. He obviously implied that at least some will not hear, which is why there are the subsequent steps.

As far as the public ministry excuse goes, this too is flawed logic, because every ministry is public, at least to some degree. Who determines the degree to which it has become so public that it frees us from compliance with God's Word? The Lord gave no such conditions. Those who take such liberties with the clear commandments given by Jesus Himself are by this logic claiming to have authority to add to the word of God. If a man we believe is in sin and has a large ministry but we are not able to get to him with our discernment, then we must not be the one to bring the judgment. Then do not accuse—intercede! The Lord is able to judge His own house and He is able to make a way for us if we are the ones He wants to use. If He does not make a way for us, we must trust Him to do it in His own time. Again, this is to protect us from coming under a judgment that is more severe than the brother who is in sin.

If we have not followed the Lord's prescribed manner for dealing with a brother who is in sin we have absolutely no right to talk about it to anyone else, much less to go public with it. It should not even be shared to get another's opinion on the matter. What we may call getting someone else's opinion God usually calls gossip. He is not fooled and we will pay the price for such indiscretions. Even if we follow all of the steps in Matthew 18 and determine that we must bring an issue before the church, our goal must always be to save the brother from his sin, not just to expose him.

Love Covers Sin

And let us not become petty with our challenges to the presumed sin in a brother's life. "...**Love covers a multitude of sins**" **(I Peter 4:8).** The majority of us still have a few hundred things wrong with us. The Lord is usually dealing with one or two of them at a time because that is all we can take. It is one of Satan's strategies to try and distract us into trying to deal with the other three hundred problems, resulting in frustration and defeat. Matthew 18 was not given to us to use as a club for beating up on each other, or even for letting a brother know how he offended us. If we have love we will cover most of those sins, unless they are bringing unnecessary injury to our brother. We must use this Scripture, and indeed all Scripture in love, not out of self-preservation or retaliation.

Of course, the Lord Jesus Himself is our perfect model. When He corrected the seven churches in Revelation, He gave us an example for bringing correction in the church. He first praised each church and highlighted what they were doing right. He then straightforwardly addressed their problems. Incredibly, He even gave Jezebel time to repent! He then gave each church a wonderful promise of reward for overcoming their problems. The Lord never changes. When He brings correction today it always comes wrapped in encouragement, hope and promises.

The "accuser of the brethren" is also trying to bring correction to the church. His methods and his goals are obviously quite different. Jesus encourages and gives hope; Satan condemns and tries to impart hopelessness. Jesus builds us up, so we can handle the correction; Satan tears us down, trying to get us to quit. Jesus loves us and wants to lift us up; Satan's goal is always destruction.

Discernment

Criticism can be rooted in true discernment. Those we criticize may well be in error. The pastors mentioned previously who criticized the way others raised money through manipulation, hype, and sometimes outright deception, were accurate in their discernment. We must walk in discernment, as Paul declared, "**...Do you not judge** those who are within the church?" (I Corinthians 5:12). The issue is how we deal with what we discern—are we going to use it to accuse or to intercede? Which ministry are we going to be a part of? How we deal with discernment can determine the outcome of our own spiritual lives.

> **A worthless person, a wicked man, walks with a perverse mouth;**

> **he winks with his eyes, he shuffles his feet, he points with his fingers;**

> **perversity is in his heart. He devises evil continually, he sows discord.**

> **Therefore his calamity shall come suddenly; suddenly he shall be broken without remedy (Proverbs 6:12-15 NKJV).**

Much of what has been paraded as discernment is nothing less than suspicion—a pseudo-spiritual disguise used to mask territorial preservation. Even without the spiritual gift of discernment, James gave us clear guidelines for discerning the source of wisdom, which, if we had heeded, would have preserved the church from some of our most humiliating failures:

> **Who is wise and understanding among you? Let him show by good**

conduct that his works are done in the meekness of wisdom.

But if you have bitter envy and self-seeking in your hearts, do not boast and lie against the truth.

This wisdom does not descend from above, but is earthly, sensual, demonic.

For where envy and self-seeking exist, confusion and every evil thing are there.

But the wisdom that is from above is first pure, then peaceable, gentle, willing to yield, full of mercy and good fruits, without partiality and without hypocrisy.

Now the fruit of righteousness is sown in peace by those who make peace (James 3:13-18 NKJV).

We are saved by grace, and we will need all of the grace that we can get to make it through this life. If we want to receive grace we had better learn to give grace, because we are going to reap what we sow. If we expect to receive mercy we must start sowing mercy, and most of us are going to need all of the mercy we can get. The very last thing we want to do is come before the Lord on that day with our brother's blood on our hands, just as He warned:

You have heard that it was said to those of old, "You shall not murder, and whoever murders will be in danger of the judgment."

But I say to you that whoever is angry with his brother without a cause shall be in danger of the judgment. And whoever says to his brother, "Raca!" [empty head] shall be in danger of the council. But whoever says, "You fool!" shall be in danger of hell fire.

Therefore if you bring your gift to the altar, and there remember that your brother has something against you,

leave your gift there before the altar, and go your way. First be reconciled to your brother, and then come and offer your gift.

Agree with your adversary quickly, while you are on the way with him, lest your adversary deliver you to the judge, the judge hand you over to the officer, and you be thrown into prison [bondage].

Assuredly, I say to you, you will by no means get out of there till you have paid the last penny (Matthew 5:21-26 NKJV).

It is clear by this warning that if we have been guilty of slandering a brother, we should forget about our offerings to the Lord until we have been reconciled to our brother. He links these together because we often think that our sacrifices and offerings can compensate for such sins, but they never will. We will stay in the prisons we make for ourselves with our judgments until we have paid the last cent, *or* until we are reconciled to the brother we slandered.

The Lord said that when He returned He was going to judge between the sheep and the goats (see Matthew 25:31-46). Those who are judged sheep will inherit the kingdom and eternal life. Those who are designated goats will be sent to eternal judgment. The separation will be determined by how each group has treated the Lord, which will be determined by how they have treated His people. John stated it:

> **If someone says, "I love God," and hates his brother, he is a liar; for the one who does not love his brother whom he has seen, cannot love God whom he has not seen (I John 4:20).**

> **Everyone who hates his brother is a murderer; and you know that no murderer has eternal life abiding in him.**

We know love by this, that He laid down His life for us; and we ought to lay down our lives for the brethren (I John 3:15-16).

If we really have Christ's Spirit, we will also have His nature. How many of us, knowing that our best friends, whom we had poured our lives into for three and a half years, were about to desert us and even deny that they knew us, would have "earnestly desired" to have one last meal with them? Our Lord's love for His disciples has never been conditional on their doing right. Even though He knew they were about to desert Him and deny Him, He loved them to the end—He even gave His life for them. When He saw our sin He did not criticize us; He laid down His life for us. He has commanded us to love with that same love.

War Between Spiritual Generations

One of the great tragedies of church history has been the way leaders of each move of God have become opposers and persecutors of succeeding moves. To date this trend has not failed. The Lord uses this to help purify and work humility into those He is about to release with increasing power and authority, but this is still a great tragedy. Numerous leaders have spent their lives serving faithfully only to finish as vessels for the accuser, who makes them a stumbling block for the next move.

What is it that causes leaders of one move to become opposers of the next move? There are several factors involved, which we must understand and be delivered of or we will end up doing the same thing. We may think and say that we would never do this, but that is what everyone has thought and said who has ended up doing it. **"Therefore let him who thinks he stands take heed lest he fall" (I Corinthians 10:12).** The pride that causes us to assume we will not do a thing is one of the factors that leads to doing it.

This problem actually precedes church history and goes all the way back to the very first two brothers born into this world. John observed why the older could not bear the younger:

> **For this is the message which you have heard from the beginning, that we should love one another;**
>
> *Not as Cain, who was of the evil one, and slew his brother. And for what reason did he slay him? Because his deeds were evil, and his brother's were righteous* (I John 3:11-12).

Each new move of the Holy Spirit has resulted in the restoration of more light to the church. This light is not new truth, but truth that was lost by the church through the Dark Ages of her history. Regardless of what we call our opposition, this is a basic reason for most of it is jealousy. Those in leadership, or those who have been faithful to the light they have had for a time, have difficulty believing that anyone is more worthy, or that the Lord would want to use anyone but them for further restoration of His truth and purposes.

The only remedy leaders have to keep them from ultimately falling to this terrible trap is to seek the humility and nature of John the Baptist. This man is one of the greatest types of true spiritual ministry. His whole purpose in life was to prepare the way for Jesus, to point to Him, then to decrease as the greater One increased. It was John's joy to see the one who followed him going further than he went.

Part IV

The Foundation Of True Ministry

True spiritual leaders must become "spiritual eunuchs." A eunuch's whole purpose was to prepare the bride for the king. It was not even possible for the eunuch to desire the bride, but his whole joy was in his king's joy. When we use the ministry in order to build a reputation, to find those who will serve us, we will not be of the authority of Christ. Paul exhorted us:

Do nothing from selfishness or empty conceit, but with humility of mind let each of you regard one another as more important than himself;

do not merely look out for your own personal interests, but also for the interests of others.

Have this attitude in yourselves which was also in Christ Jesus,

who, although He existed in the form of God, did not regard equality with God a thing to be grasped,

but emptied Himself, taking the form of a bond-servant, and being made in the likeness of men.

And being found in appearance as a man, He humbled Himself by becoming obedient to the point of death, even death on a cross.

Therefore also God highly exalted Him, and bestowed on Him the name which is above every name (Philippians 2:3-9).

This is the pattern that Jesus set for everyone who would follow Him in leadership. Humility comes before authority and position. He said in Luke 14:11: **"For everyone who exalts himself shall be humbled, and he who humbles himself shall be exalted."** A key word here is "everyone." James added, **"Humble yourselves in the presence of the Lord, and He will exalt you" (James 4:10).** Peter stated: **"Humble yourselves, therefore, under the mighty hand of God, that He may exalt you at the proper time (I Peter 5:6).** In all of these texts we see that it is our job to humble ourselves and it is the Lord's job to do the exalting. It is clear that if we try to do His job He will do our job, and He can do either one of them much better than we can.

The evil spirits of self-promotion and territorial preservation have done much damage to the church. They have caused many potentially great leaders to be disqualified from receiving further anointing and authority. The influence that we gain by our own self-promotion or manipulation will be a stumbling block that keeps us from attaining positions that God would otherwise give to us.

It has not always been the older generation of leaders that is the stumbling block for the new. The new generation can be just as guilty of causing the previous one to stumble! The very arrogance of presuming that we are the new generation reveals a pride that God has to resist. This is a humiliating slap in the face to men and women who have given their lives to faithfully serving the Lord and His people.

Jesus did not ridicule John the Baptist for being a part of the old order—He honored him. Jesus even submitted Himself to John's ministry. This submission did not mean that He allowed John to control Him, but He acknowledged John and esteemed him and his work.

Later, when Jesus was asked the source of His authority, he pointed to John and asked His inquisitors if they knew from where John's baptism had come. The answer to that question was the answer to their question. John was the last of an order; he was there to represent all of those who had prophesied of the coming Messiah from the very beginning. John was their representative to acknowledge Jesus as the One of whom they had all spoken, that He was indeed the Lamb of God. Jesus acknowledged the baptism of those who had gone before Him as the credentials of His authority.

Those who will be of the new generation must likewise submit to the ministry of all of those who have gone before them if they are to fulfill all righteousness. We are presently in the midst of seeing a new spiritual generation emerge. It is also apparent that the previous movements are beginning to decrease as the new order emerges. However, it is crucial that the leaders of the new order honor those who went before them, or they will be in jeopardy of disqualifying themselves from going further. The arrogance of the new order can be just as much an affront to the Spirit of God as that of the old who start to resist God in the new things He begins to do.

Why the Abused Become Abusers

Why is it that abused children grow up to be abusers? Why is it that accused saints grow up to become accusers? The answer is the same for both. Abused children usually grow up determined not to be like their parents, so they become reactionary, which does not lead to grace, but can actually nurture bitterness. This ultimately results in their becoming just like their parents. Only humility and forgiveness will ever break that cycle. The sins of the parents will become the sins of the children until we receive the grace of the cross. Because God gives grace to the humble, we must understand that we will take on the sins of our parents without His help. That is one reason why many of the great leaders in Scripture prayed to be forgiven for the sins of their fathers.

Elijah Must Come

There will be a spiritual generation that will be persecuted like every one has before it, but which will not go on to persecute the next generation. This movement will not have become subject to the "pride of generations," assuming that all things will be concluded with them. Those of this generation will have found the grace of the cross and will have forgiven from the heart those who mistreated them. They will also perceive and even hope that their children, spiritual and natural, may go further in Christ than they did, and they will rejoice in it. They will give their lives to make the way of that generation as smooth as possible, and then they will rejoice to decrease as that generation arises. This will be the generation of the spirit of Elijah who will return the hearts of the fathers to the sons, and the hearts of the sons to the fathers.

Our ability to be the generation that prepares the way for the Lord and His ultimate purposes will be determined by which of the two ministries we become a part of—accusation or intercession. Let us now remove the terrible yoke of "pointing the finger" from our midst and begin turning our criticisms into intercession.

Then your light will break out like the dawn, and your recovery will speedily spring forth; and your righteousness will go before you; the glory of the LORD will be your rear guard.

Then you will call, and the LORD will answer; you will cry, and He will say, "Here I am." If you remove the yoke from you midst, the pointing of the finger, and speaking wickedness.

And the LORD will continually guide you, and satisfy your desire in scorched places, and give strength to your bones; and you will be like

a watered garden, and like a spring of water whose waters do not fail.

And those from among you will rebuild the ancient ruins; you will raise up the age-old foundations; and you will be called the repairer of the breach, the restorer of the streets in which to dwell (Isaiah 58:8-9, 11-12).

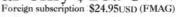